Common Core Lesson[illegible]
Underground [illegible]

By Carole Marsh

Published by Gallopade International, Inc.

Printed in the U.S.A. (Peachtree City, Georgia)

TABLE OF CONTENTS

G: Includes Graphic Organizer

GO: Graphic Organizer is also available 8½" x 11" online download at www.gallopade.com/client/go

(numbers above correspond to the graphic organizer numbers online)

The Underground Railroad

Read the text and answer the questions.

The "Underground Railroad" was not a railroad at all. The Underground Railroad was a network of people, routes, and safe places that helped enslaved people escape to freedom—usually to the Northern states and Canada. Many people, both white and Black, in the North and South, took part in this secretive effort.

The Underground Railroad was very dangerous for enslaved people escaping to freedom. Their enslavers considered them fugitives and wanted to catch and punish them. Owners placed advertisements in local newspapers, offering rewards for the capture and return of their enslaved people who had escaped.

Free Black people in the North were not safe either. After the passage of the Fugitive Slave Act in 1850, many free Black people in northern states were kidnapped and enslaved. Free Black people received very little protection from the law.

Abolitionists were people in the North and South who wanted to end slavery. Many abolitionists aided enslaved people who escaped along the Underground Railroad. But, being a part of the Underground Railroad was breaking the law, and not all abolitionists were willing to do that. Abolitionists who helped people escape risked fines and imprisonment under the Fugitive Slave Act of 1850.

To protect everyone involved in the Underground Railroad, nothing was written down. All communication was oral and spoken in secret code. Safe houses, called "stations" or "depots" were places where people fleeing slavery, called "passengers," hid, ate, and slept. These "stations" were run by "stationmasters," who were ordinary people that offered protection to those fleeing slavery. "Stockholders" were people sympathetic to the cause of ending slavery, who donated money or goods. Those who guided the "passengers" were known as "conductors." The secret paths along the Underground Railroad were called "lines." Even the railroad itself had a name: "The Freedom Train." The Underground Railroad's final destination was Canada, which many enslaved people called the "Promised Land."

PART A: Use the text to answer the vocabulary questions.

1. A. Use the text to define "Underground Railroad."
   B. What is the significance of the word "underground"?
   C. Why was it called a "railroad"?
   D. Is "Underground Railroad" figurative or literal? Explain.
   E. Why was the Underground Railroad created?
2. What is a synonym for <u>fugitives</u> as it is used in the text?
3. A. Define <u>abolitionists</u> as it is used in the text.
   B. Why were some abolitionists involved in the Underground Railroad? Why were some not involved?

PART B: Use the text to infer whether each statement is **true** or **false**. Write **T** for true and **F** for false. Then for each statement, explain "why."

4. ______ The laws against helping enslaved people discouraged some abolitionists from participating in the Underground Railroad.
5. ______ When enslaved people who had escaped reached the Northern free states, they were safe from capture.
6. ______ The Fugitive Slave Act made the journey to freedom easier.
7. ______ Slave catchers were not allowed to search for formerly enslaved people in Canada.

PART C: Use the text to complete the graphic organizer by identifying the people and places of the Underground Railroad.

Friends of the Underground Railroad

Read the text and answer the questions.

Conductors were the men and women, both Black and white, who guided enslaved people from one safe station (hiding place) to the next on the Underground Railroad. Conductors often traveled with the enslaved people and shared their knowledge of safe passages.

The most famous conductor was Harriet Tubman. Harriet Tubman was born into slavery and escaped to the North as a young woman. She returned to the South, at great risk to herself, and led her family to freedom. Tubman made 19 journeys on the Underground Railroad in her lifetime, leading over 300 enslaved people to freedom. Another conductor was Samuel Burris. Burris was a Black man, but he was born free. Wanting to help others have a free life, Burris helped many enslaved people escape along the Underground Railroad in Delaware. But in Delaware, the punishment for a free Black person helping enslaved people escape was slavery itself, and Burris was caught and enslaved. Fortunately, some abolitionists "bought" Burris and set him free.

Stationmasters provided safe houses along the Underground Railroad. Stationmasters risked fines and imprisonment for helping people escaping slavery. The Quaker Society of Friends provided safe houses in many northern states. Levi and Catherine Coffin were two Quaker stationmasters who lived in the free state of Ohio. About 2,000 people fleeing slavery found shelter in the Coffin's home on their way to Canada. Thus, Levi was nicknamed "President of the Underground Railroad."

1. A. Explain the role of conductors on the Underground Railroad.
   B. Explain the role of stationmasters on the Underground Railroad.
2. Make at least three inferences about Harriet Tubman's character. Cite evidence from the text to support each inference.
3. Compare and contrast Samuel Burris and Levi Coffin in terms of the roles and risks that each took on the Underground Railroad.
4. A. What was Levi Coffin's nickname, and why was he called it?
   B. Was this nickname literal or figurative? Explain.

Underground Codes

Read the secret codes used on the Underground Railroad. Then answer the questions.

- **Agent**
  Someone who coordinates escapes for enslaved people
- **Baggage, boxes, parcel, packages, passengers**
  People fleeing slavery
- **Brakeman**
  Someone who helps people fleeing slavery find jobs and homes when they reach freedom
- **Forward**
  To move enslaved people between stations
- **Station**
  Safe place where people fleeing slavery were hidden and sheltered
- **"Lost a passenger"**
  Person fleeing slavery has been caught
- **Stationmaster**
  Someone who provides shelter for people fleeing slavery
- **"The wind blows from the South today."**
  People fleeing slavery are in the area
- **"A friend with friends"**
  A password used by a conductor arriving with people fleeing slavery
- **Moses**
  Harriet Tubman

1. Use what you know and make inferences to explain the purpose of secret codes on the Underground Railroad.
2. Use the code chart to explain each of the following messages:
   A. The wind blows from the South today. Moses will arrive at the station with baggage.
   B. I am a friend with friends. I will be forwarding 3 parcels to Philadelphia. Please inform the stationmaster there to prepare a brakeman.
3. Use the Underground Railroad code to write a your own message. In small groups, take turns reading your message aloud. Decode each person's message and explain its meaning.

PRIMARY SOURCE ANALYSIS

Narrative of Henry Bibb

As a young man enslaved in Kentucky, Henry Bibb made several unsuccessful attempts at escaping slavery. He endured harsh punishment, persisted in his pursuit of freedom, and eventually reached Canada on the Underground Railroad. The text below is an excerpt from the Narrative of the Life and Adventures of Henry Bibb.

Read the text and answer the questions.

"In the fall or winter of 1837 I formed a resolution that I would escape, if possible, to Canada, for my Liberty... My preparation for this voyage consisted in the accumulation of a little money, perhaps not exceeding two dollars and fifty cents, and a suit which I had never been seen or known to wear before; this last was to avoid detection.

On the twenty-fifth of December, 1837, my long anticipated time had arrived when I was to put into operation my former resolution, which was to bolt for Liberty or consent to die a Slave. I acted upon the former, although I confess it to be one of the most self-defying acts of my whole life, to take leave of an affectionate wife, who stood before me on my departure, with dear little Frances in her arms, and with tears of sorrow in her eyes as she bid me a long farewell. It required all the moral courage that I was master of to suppress my feelings while taking leave of my little family.

Had Matilda known my intention at the time, it would not have been possible for me to have got away, and I might have this day been a slave...[but] the voice of liberty was thundering in my very soul, 'Be free, oh, man! be free.' I was struggling against a thousand obstacles which had clustered around my mind to bind my wounded spirit... My strong attachments to friends and relatives, with all the love of home and birth-place which is so natural among the human family, twined about my heart and were hard to break away from. And withal, the fear of being killed, or captured and taken to the extreme South, to linger out my days in hopeless bondage on some cotton or sugar plantation, all combined to deter me. But I had count the cost, and was fully prepared to make the sacrifice. The time for fulfilling my pledge was then at hand. I must forsake friends and neighbors, wife and child, or consent to live and die a slave."

PART A: Use the text to answer the questions.

1. Make at least 3-5 inferences about the author of this text.
2. Write an appropriate title to express the main idea of this text.
3. Describe Henry Bibb's attitude toward family. Cite evidence from the text to support your description.
4. Describe Henry Bibb's attitude toward freedom. Cite evidence from the text to support your description.
5. Why does Henry Bibb choose to run to freedom?
6. Why does Bibb describe his decision as "one of the most self-defying acts of my life"?

PART B: Analyze the context of each phrase in the text to identify what is being described.

7. "formed a resolution" in the first paragraph
8. "bolt for Liberty" in the second paragraph
9. "the voice of liberty" in the third paragraph
10. "hopeless bondage" in the third paragraph

PART C: Compete the graphic organizer by listing the positive and negative aspects of escaping, as described by Henry Bibb.

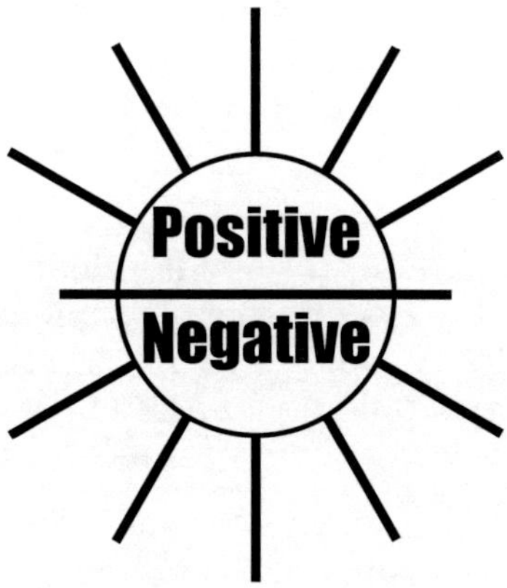

A Difficult Decision

Read the text and answer the questions.

1) The decision to attempt to escape slavery was not an easy one to make. Many factors deterred most enslaved people from running away.

2) Enslaved people understood that if they decided to run away, the journey to freedom would be perilous. In order to avoid detection, they traveled at night. They rarely had maps and relied on the stars and word-of-mouth to find their way. They were exposed to the elements outdoors, with no assurance of shelter. They crossed hundreds of miles, often on foot. Finding food was difficult, and hunger was the norm.

3) In addition to risking life and limb, abandoning friends and family in the South was an even greater personal obstacle. Few enslaved people were willing to leave their families, but the difficulty of the journey meant it was rarely feasible for a whole family to attempt escape together. Women and children, as well as anyone sickly or elderly, often had little chance of survival and success.

4) The consequences of capture were a huge risk of escaping. Slave owners offered rewards for the return of enslaved people who escaped, making it hard for people fleeing slavery to know whom to trust. If caught, people fleeing slavery faced severe punishments from their enslavers who wished to discourage others from attempting escape. Enslaved people knew that an unsuccessful attempt at escape could result in a life worse than the one they wanted to flee.

5) Enslaved people knew they would face uncertainties and difficulties even if they were successful in their attempt to escape. Starting a new life in the North brought many unknowns. Upon reaching the North, they would have no friends, no job, and no way to make a living. They would be far away from the only life they had ever known. This was a scary prospect for many.

6) The physical danger they would face, the loss of family and friends, the risks and punishments if caught, and the uncertainty of the new life they would lead if they succeeded in escaping were all deterrents from trying to escape. Despite the many obstacles, many enslaved people did decide to try to escape.

PART A: Use the text to answer the following questions.

1. A. Summarize the main idea of the text.
   B. Describe how the main idea is developed and supported.
2. Did most enslaved people attempt to escape? Why or why not?
3. Use the text and make inferences to list at least three ways that enslaved people would likely have been aware of the risks of trying to escape.

PART B: Read each primary source excerpt and answer the questions.

> "They hide themselves during the day in the woods and swamps; at night they travel, crossing rivers by swimming, or by boats they may chance to meet with... in these dangerous journeys they are guided by the north-star... They subsist on such wild fruit as they can gather, and as they are often very long on their way, they reach the free states almost like skeletons."

4. This primary source best supports which paragraph of the text?
5. Compare and contrast the excerpt and the corresponding paragraph. Include content, point of view, style, effectiveness, and other factors.
6. Why did enslaved people often reach the free states "almost like skeletons"? Cite evidence from the text and primary source.

> "...an intelligent, bright girl, 21 years age. Five feet four inches high…She has a decayed spot on a front tooth…All persons are forbidden, under penalty of the law, to harbor or employ said slave. $150 will be given to whoever takes her in the state, and $300 if taken out of the state..."

7. This primary source best supports which paragraph of the text?
8. Make 2-3 inferences about the author of the primary source. Cite evidence from the primary source or text to support each inference.
9. Who was the intended audience of the primary source?
10. What effects might this excerpt have on a person fleeing slavery? Cite evidence from the text to support your answer.

> "I made up my mind that I did not want to be sold like a horse... I resolved to die sooner than I would be taken back."

11. This primary source best supports which paragraph of the text?
12. Make 3-5 inferences about the author of the primary source.

DATA ANALYSIS

Cotton Production

Read the text, look at the charts, and answer the questions.

The invention of the cotton gin in the late 1700s allowed cotton to be produced more efficiently. The development of the textile industry in the early 1800s increased demand for cotton.

U.S. Cotton Production

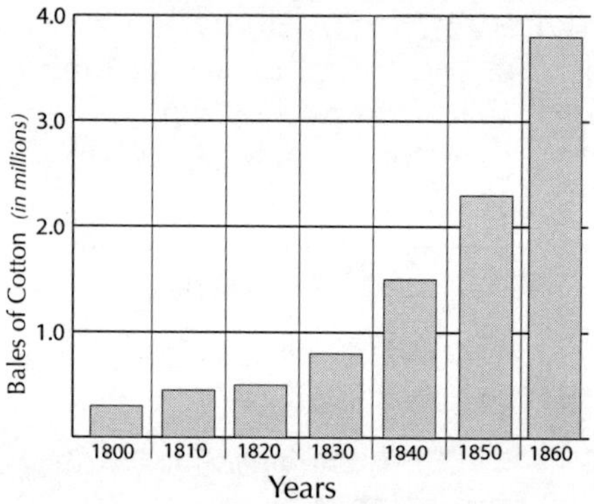

U.S. Slave Population

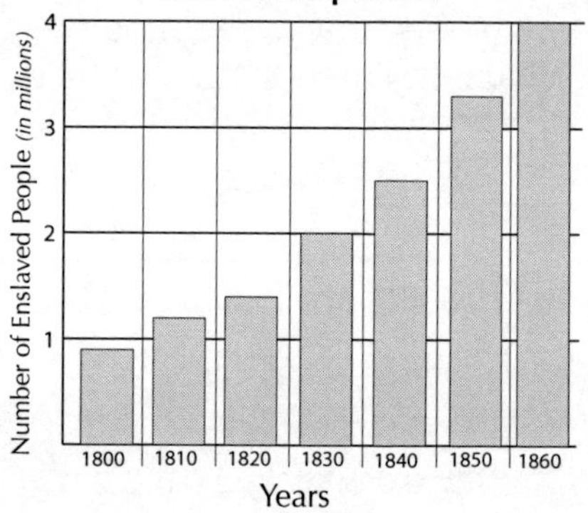

1. How did cotton production change from 1800 to 1860?
2. How did the number of enslaved people change from 1800 to 1860?
3. What is the relationship between the amount of cotton produced and the number of enslaved people?
4. In what year did cotton production total more than one million bales?
5. In what year did the number of enslaved people reach 4 million?
6. How might an enslaved person or an abolitionist have felt about the invention of the cotton gin and the development of the textile industry?

MAP ACTIVITY

Railroad Routes

Look at the map and answer the questions.

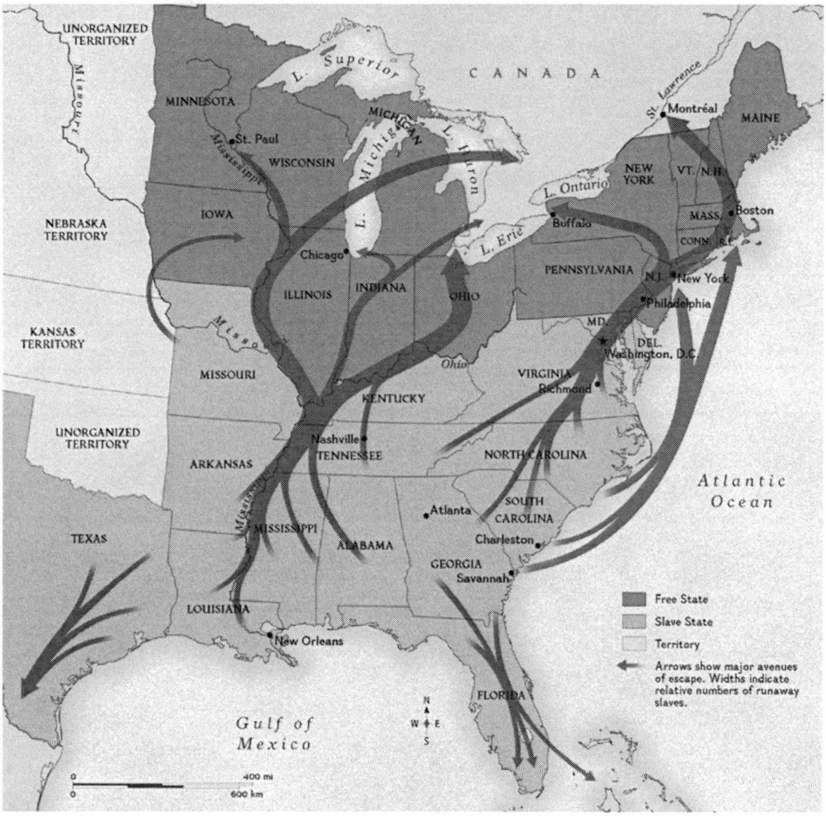

1. What information does this map present?
2. A. In what states did the Underground Railroad begin?
   B. Where did most Underground Railroad routes lead? Why?
3. Most people fleeing slavery from Alabama and Mississippi followed what geographic features?
4. **True** or **False**: Enslaved people only sought freedom in the North. Explain.
5. A. Estimate the approximate time period this map represents.
   B. Cite at least two things from the map to support your conclusion.

Tracks of the Underground Railroad

Complete the chart by identifying the purpose of each participant in the Underground Railroad. Then complete the graphic organizer by identifying the problems faced by people fleeing slavery on each phase of the journey and the people and solutions that helped them.

Key Participants	Purpose
Conductors	
Enslaved people	
Stationmasters	
Stockholders	
Abolitionists	

Life in Slavery

Problems:

Solutions/Help:

Riding the Railroad

Problems:

Solutions/Help:

Living in the North

Problems:

Solutions/Help:

COMPARE & CONTRAST

Surprising Escapes

Read the following accounts of escape (retold in the first person). Then answer the questions.

Henry "Box" Brown

I was born into slavery, but I was never deprived of clothes or food, and although I was occasionally punished, it was never severe. Yet, I longed for freedom.

Before the Civil War, I escaped slavery in a wooden box! My white abolitionist friend, Samuel A. Smith, packed me in a wooden crate, and off I went on a 27-hour journey, from Richmond, Virginia, to William Still in Philadelphia, Pennsylvania. I arrived safely, though a little wet. So happy was I, I burst out singing!

Harriet Jacobs

I had a happy childhood. My mistress cared for me as if I were her family. When my mother died, my mistress even taught me to read and sew. When I was only 12 years old, my beloved mistress died, and I was given to Mr. James Norcom. Mr. Norcom was abusive and ill-tempered. I attempted to marry a white lawyer from town, but my master refused, even when I had two children by the lawyer. Mr. Norcom set his heart on working my children as slaves on his plantation.

I ran away, but lacking the means to travel, I was forced to hide in a tiny crawlspace above my grandmother's porch. I could barely move, and mice and rats crawled on my body. Through a tiny peephole, I could see my children play outside, but I could not return to them—I feared the violent hand of my master. I stayed silent in my tiny prison for 7 long years, eating small rations fed to me at night, until I could secure passage North. Finally the day came, and I made my escape by boat to Philadelphia.

1. Compare and contrast Brown and Jacobs' motivations for escape.
2. Compare and contrast the escape experiences of Brown and Jacobs.
3. How were Harriet Jacobs' two enslavers similar? How were they different? Cite evidence from the text to support your answers.

Escape Quotations

Read each quotation and complete the chart. Then answer the questions.

Quotations:	What part of the journey is represented by each quotation? Explain.
"I clasped this money, realizing that I had no master who could take it from me,—*that it was mine—that my hands were my own, and could earn more of the precious coin...*"	
"I had crossed the line. I was free; but there was no one to welcome me to the land of freedom. I was a stranger in a strange land."	
"I had reasoned this out in my mind, there was one of two things I had the right to, liberty or death. If I could not have one, I would have the other."	

1. Explain why the ability to earn money was important to people escaping slavery.
2. Match the quotation (1, 2, or 3) to the word that best represents the experience described in the quotation. Use a dictionary if needed.
   A. _____ isolation
   B. _____ determination
   C. _____ elation
3. Describe the range of emotions someone might experience while traveling on the Underground Railroad. Think about what you have learned and cite evidence from the quotations to support your response.

The Fugitive Slave Act

The Fugitive Slave Act of 1850 gave slave owners the right to pursue and re-enslave those who had escaped. It also penalized people who helped those escaping to freedom.

Look at the poster and answer the questions.

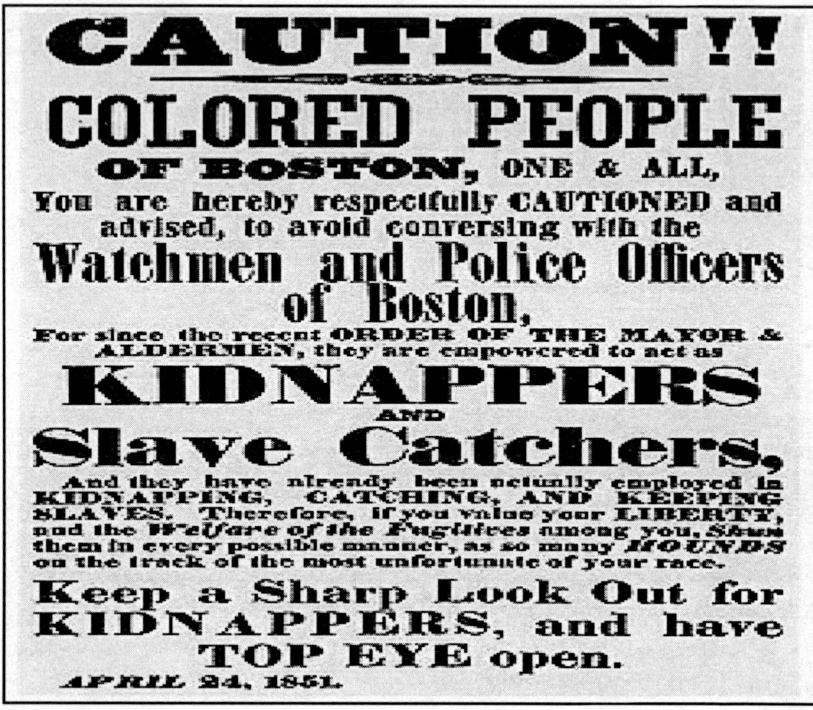

CAUTION!!

COLORED PEOPLE

OF BOSTON, ONE & ALL,

You are hereby respectfully CAUTIONED and advised, to avoid conversing with the

Watchmen and Police Officers of Boston,

For since the recent ORDER OF THE MAYOR & ALDERMEN, they are empowered to act as

KIDNAPPERS

AND

Slave Catchers,

And they have already been actually employed in KIDNAPPING, CATCHING, AND KEEPING SLAVES. Therefore, if you value your LIBERTY, and the *Welfare of the Fugitives* among you, *Shun* them in every possible manner, as so many *HOUNDS* on the track of the most unfortunate of your race.

Keep a Sharp Look Out for KIDNAPPERS, and have TOP EYE open.

APRIL 24, 1851.

Courtesy of Wikipedia

1. Who is the intended audience of this poster? Cite evidence from the poster to support your conclusion.
2. Summarize the primary message of this poster.
3. A. Does this poster **support** or **oppose** the Fugitive Slave Act? How do you know?
   B. What can you infer about the author of this poster? Explain.
4. In your opinion, is this poster effective? Why or why not?
5. Write a paragraph describing your reaction to this poster from the perspective of an abolitionist, slave owner, or enslaved person. Read your response aloud. Can your audience accurately determine your point of view?

PRIMARY SOURCE ANALYSIS

Captured!

Read the text and answer the questions.

This narrative by an enslaved person appeared in *The Liberator,* March 9, 1855.

[When I escaped to Boston], I didn't want to make myself known, so I didn't tell who I was; but as I came to work, I got employment, and I worked hard; but I kept my own counsel, and didn't tell anybody that I was a slave, but I strove for myself as I never had an opportunity to do before.

When I was going home one night I heard some one running behind me; presently a hand was put on my shoulder, and somebody said: "Stop, stop; you are the fellow who broke into a silversmith's shop the other night." I assured the man that it was a mistake, but almost before I could speak, I was lifted from off my feet by six or seven others, and it was no use to resist. In the Court House I waited some time, and as the silversmith did not come, I told them I wanted to go home for supper. A man then come to the door; he didn't open it like an honest man would, but kind of slowly opened it, and looked in. He said, "How do you do, Mr. Burns?" and I called him as we do in Virginia, "master!"...

The next morning they told me that my master said that he had the right to me, and as I had called him "master," having the fear of God before my eyes, I could not go from it. Next morning I was taken down, with the bracelets on my wrists—not such as you wear, ladies, of gold and silver -- but iron and steel, that wore into the bone.

1. Make at least three inferences about the author of this story.
2. A. On what charge is the author arrested?
   B. What is the underlying motivation for arresting the author?
3. A. How does the author characterize himself? Why?
   B. How does the author characterize his master? Why?
   C. What is the author's purpose in telling this story?
4. Which group of people best represents the intended audience of this story? Cite evidence from the text to explain your choice.
   A. enslaved people B. free Black people C. Northern white people

CAUSE & EFFECT

The North Changes

Read the text and answer the questions.

The North was a hard place for Black people. They were wrongly viewed as an inferior race by many white people, they did not have as many rights and opportunities as white people, they had to work hard, and were often poor (as was true for many white people). But, for enslaved people, Northern states represented freedom. The North was a place they would be free, a place they would be paid for the work they did, and a place where they could not be beaten or forced apart from their family.

However, once the Fugitive Slave Act of 1850 was passed, the North became an even riskier place for Black people to live. The Fugitive Slave Act issued harsh penalties for helping people escape slavery. The act permitted slave catchers to search for people fleeing slavery in free Northern states, and it authorized government officials to return people fleeing slavery quickly to the South. Additionally, the North became unsafe for free Black people as well, because they could be accused of being a runaway and sent South before they had a chance to prove they were free!

Despite all of this, the Fugitive Slave Act of 1850 actually helped change Northern opinion about slavery. Why? Many white people in the North had never seen slavery, and so they viewed it as a Southern problem. The Fugitive Slave Act allowed their homes to be searched for people fleeing slavery, punished those who helped people escape slavery, and exposed the cruel treatment of enslaved people. In effect, the impact of slavery became close and personal to many Northern white people. No longer was the North quite so removed from slavery– some aspects of slavery had been forced into their free Northern states and into their lives.

1. Why did many enslaved people want to escape to the North? Explain.
2. Use the text and make inferences to create a table and explain the effects of the Fugitive Slave Act of 1850 on each group of people:
   A. Free Black people in the North
   B. White people in the North
   C. Slave owners in the South
   D. Enslaved people in the South

PRIMARY SOURCE ANALYSIS

Song of the Free

The following three stanzas are from the "Song of the Free," written in 1860.

Read the text and answer the questions.

1

I served my master all my days
Without a dime's reward,

But now I'm forced to run away
To flee the lash abhorred,

The hounds are baying on my track
The master just behind,

Resolved that he will bring me back
Before I cross the line.

Oh, old master don't come after me
I'm going up to Canada where colored
men are free.

2

Ohio's not the place for me,
For I was much surprised,

So many of her sons to see
In garments of disguise;

Her name has gone throughout the world
Free labor, soil and men,

But slaves had better far be hurled
Into a lion's den.

Farewell Ohio, I'm not safe in thee,
I'll travel on to Canada where
colored men are free.

3

I've landed safe in Canada,
Both soul and body free,

My blood and brains and tears no more
Shall drench old Tennessee;

Yet I behold the scalding tears
Now streaming from my eye,

To think my wife, my only dear,
A slave must live and die.

Oh, Susannah, don't grieve after me,
Forever at the throne of God, I will remember
thee.

1. A. From what point of view is the text written?
   B. How does the point of view differ slightly between each stanza?
2. Match the following questions to whether they are best answered by stanza 1, 2, or 3.
   A. _____ Why did many people fleeing slavery continue traveling to Canada rather than staying in free states in the North?
   B. _____ What was life like for enslaved people?
   C. _____ What was often the personal cost of freedom?
3. Cite directly from the text to provide examples or answers for A-C.
   A. Two reasons enslaved people attempted to escape
   B. Three perils enslaved people faced while escaping
   C. One reason enslaved people tried to reach Canada

The Power of the Pen

Read the text and answer the questions.

In the 1840s and 1850s, not too many white Northerners supported the end, or abolition, of slavery. In order to change this, abolitionists used "the power of the pen" to inform Northerners and to change their opinion about slavery. Abolitionists used books, pamphlets, sermons, lectures, newspapers, and narratives by enslaved people to spread their anti-slavery message. "The power of the pen" increased the conflict over slavery between North and South.

Narratives by enslaved people were first-hand accounts of what it was like to live in slavery. Formerly enslaved people told stories about their love for family members, their bonds with friends, and their desires for freedom and education. They told of the terrible conditions of slavery, of families being separated, and of free Black people being kidnapped. Formerly enslaved people often told their personal stories aloud at anti-slavery meetings or published them in anti-slavery newspapers such as William Lloyd Garrison's *The Liberator* or Frederick Douglass' *North Star*. For many Northerners, the effect of hearing horrific stories of slavery was eye-opening.

Such narratives were incredibly popular in the North. People who had escaped slavery such as Frederick Douglass, Sojourner Truth, and William Wells Brown became famous by sharing their experiences and their inspiring journeys to freedom. Douglass' autobiography sold over 30,000 copies between 1845 and 1860. Samuel Northrop's *Twelve Years as a Slave* sold 27,000 copies in its first two years.

Despite the popularity of these real narratives, it was Harriet Beecher Stowe's fictional novel *Uncle Tom's Cabin* that won the most Northerners to the abolition movement. Stowe depicted the main character, Uncle Tom, as a kindly old enslaved man. In the face of great hardship, Uncle Tom remains a strong Christian man who is a loyal friend. In contrast, Uncle Tom's master is a cruel slave dealer. Stowe's novel caused readers to sympathize with Uncle Tom, and thus, recognize the evils of slavery. *Uncle Tom's Cabin* sold over 300,000 copies in the first year, and convinced many Northerners to support the abolitionist movement.

PART A: Use the text to answer the questions.

1. A. Use the text to define <u>abolitionists</u>.
   B. Use the text to explain the meaning of "the power of the pen."
   C. Explain the relationship between <u>abolitionists</u> and "the power of the pen" as described in the text.
   D. Was "the power of the pen" effective for abolitionists? Cite specific examples from the text to explain why or why not.
   E. How did the number of abolitionists change in the 1850s? Why?
2. List five characteristics of a narrative written by an enslaved person.
3. A. Use the text to define <u>eye-opening</u>.
   B. Why were the stories of enslaved people "eye opening" for many Northerners?
4. The Civil War between the North and South began in 1861. In 1862, President Abraham Lincoln met Harriet Beecher Stowe, and greeted her by saying, "So you're the little woman who wrote the book that made this great war!" Explain what Lincoln meant by his statement.

PART B: Use the text to complete the graphic organizers.

5. Complete the graphic organizer by identifying several ways that abolitionists used the "power of the pen."

6. Complete the graphic organizer to show the effects of abolitionists' use of "the power of the pen."

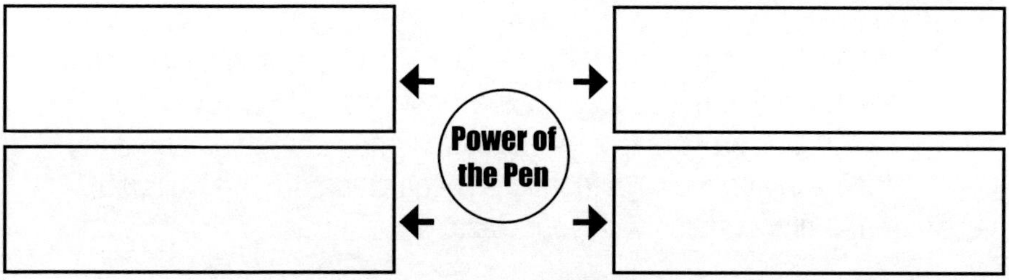

Influential People

Use what you know and other resources to complete the graphic organizer summarizing each person's influence and role related to the Underground Railroad.

People:	Who am I?	What did I do?
Harriet Tubman		
William Still		
John Brown		
Frederick Douglass		
John Fairfield		
Levi Coffin		
William Lloyd Garrison		
Josiah Henson		
John Brown		
Dred Scott		
Abraham Lincoln		

Writing Prompt

A. Use at least two online resources to do further research on one person who was important to the success of the Underground Railroad.
B. Create a digital presentation with pictures and information about the person, their life, and their contributions to the Underground Railroad.
C. Share the presentation with your class.

Underground Railroad Vocabulary

Use a dictionary and other resources to complete the graphic organizer for each vocabulary word.

abolitionist	enslaved	fugitive	slave auction
conductor	free state	plantation	slave state
courage	freedom	property	slave trade

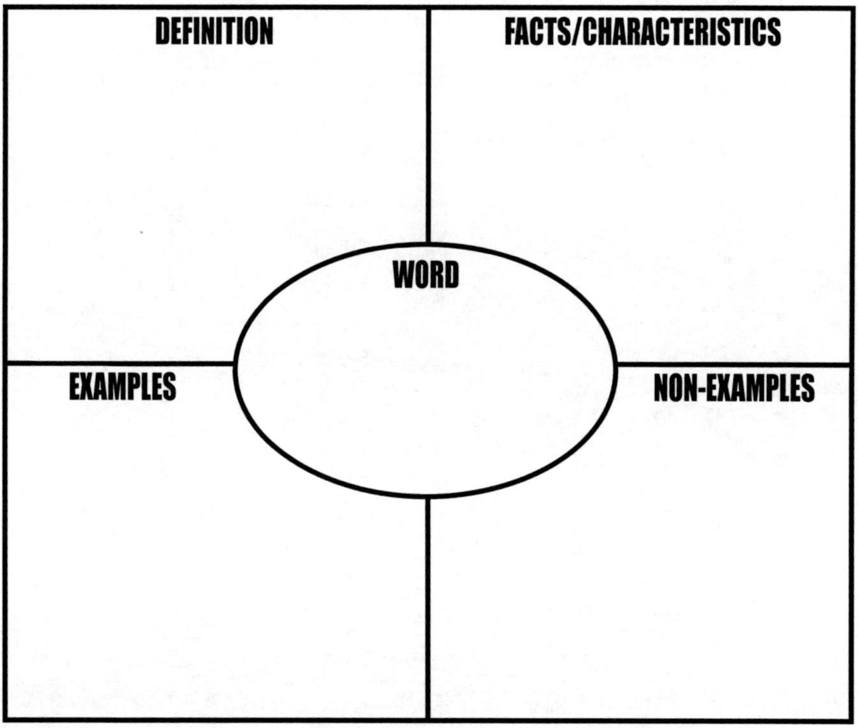

Explain what each of the following is and how it relates to the Underground Railroad.

1. cotton gin
2. Emancipation Proclamation
3. *Uncle Tom's Cabin*
4. *The Liberator*
5. *North Star*

Correlations to Common Core State Standards

For your convenience, correlations are listed page-by-page, and for the entire book!

This book is correlated to the Common Core State Standards for English Language Arts grades 3-8, and to Common Core State Standards for Literacy in History, Science, & Technological Subjects grades 6-8.

Correlations are highlighted in gray.

PAGE #	READING *Includes:* RI: Reading Informational Text RH: Reading History/Social Studies	WRITING *Includes:* W: Writing WHST: Writing History/Social Studies, Science, & Technical Subjects	LANGUAGE *Includes:* L: Language LF: Language Foundational Skills	SPEAKING & LISTENING *Includes:* SL: Speaking & Listening
2-3	RI RH . **1** **2** **3** **4** **5** 6 7 **8** 9 **10**	W WHST . 1 **2** 3 **4** 5 6 7 **8** **9** **10**	L LF . 1 2 **3** **4** **5** **6**	SL . 1 2 3 4 5 6
4	RI RH . **1** 2 **3** **4** **5** 6 7 **8** 9 **10**	W WHST . 1 **2** 3 **4** 5 6 7 **8** **9** **10**	L LF . 1 2 **3** **4** **5** **6**	SL . 1 2 3 4 5 6
5	RI RH . **1** **2** **3** **4** **5** 6 **7** 8 **9** **10**	W WHST . **1** **2** 3 **4** **5** 6 7 **8** 9 **10**	L LF . 1 **2** 3 **4** **5** **6**	SL . **1** **2** 3 4 5 **6**
6-7	RI RH . **1** **2** **3** **4** **5** 6 7 **8** 9 **10**	W WHST . **1** **2** 3 **4** **5** 6 7 **8** **9** **10**	L LF . 1 2 3 **4** **5** **6**	SL . 1 2 3 4 5 6
8-9	RI RH . **1** **2** **3** **4** **5** **6** 7 **8** **9** **10**	W WHST . 1 **2** 3 **4** 5 6 7 8 **9** **10**	L LF . 1 2 3 **4** 5 **6**	SL . 1 2 3 4 5 6
10	RI RH . **1** **2** **3** **4** **5** **6** **7** 8 **9** **10**	W WHST . 1 **2** 3 **4** 5 6 7 8 9 10	L LF . 1 2 3 **4** **5** **6**	SL . 1 2 3 4 5 6
11	RI RH . **1** 2 **3** 4 **5** 6 **7** 8 9 **10**	W WHST . 1 **2** 3 **4** 5 6 7 8 9 10	L LF . 1 2 3 4 5 6	SL . 1 2 3 4 5 6
12-13	RI RH . **1** **2** **3** 4 **5** 6 **7** 8 9 **10**	W WHST . 1 **2** **3** **4** **5** 6 **7** **8** **9** **10**	L LF . 1 **2** **3** 4 **5** 6	SL . **1** **2** 3 4 **5** 6
14	RI RH . **1** 2 **3** 4 **5** **6** 7 8 **9** **10**	W WHST . 1 **2** 3 **4** 5 6 7 8 **9** **10**	L LF . 1 2 3 **4** 5 6	SL . 1 2 3 4 5 6
15	RI RH . **1** **2** **3** 4 **5** 6 **7** **8** **9** **10**	W WHST . **1** **2** **3** **4** 5 6 7 **8** 9 **10**	L LF . 1 2 3 **4** **5** **6**	SL . 1 2 3 4 5 6
16	RI RH . **1** **2** **3** **4** **5** 6 **7** **8** 9 **10**	W WHST . **1** **2** 3 **4** 5 6 7 **8** **9** **10**	L LF . 1 2 3 **4** 5 **6**	SL . **1** **2** 3 **4** 5 **6**
17	RI RH . **1** **2** **3** **4** **5** 6 7 **8** 9 **10**	W WHST . 1 **2** 3 **4** 5 6 7 **8** **9** **10**	L LF . 1 2 3 **4** 5 **6**	SL . 1 2 3 4 5 6
18	RI RH . **1** 2 **3** 4 **5** 6 **7** 8 9 **10**	W WHST . 1 **2** 3 **4** **5** 6 7 **8** 9 **10**	L LF . 1 2 3 4 5 6	SL . 1 2 3 4 5 6
19	RI RH . **1** **2** **3** 4 **5** **6** 7 **8** 9 **10**	W WHST . **1** **2** 3 **4** 5 6 7 **8** **9** **10**	L LF . 1 2 3 **4** **5** **6**	SL . 1 2 3 4 5 6
20-21	RI RH . **1** **2** **3** **4** **5** 6 7 **8** 9 **10**	W WHST . 1 **2** 3 **4** **5** 6 7 **8** 9 **10**	L LF . 1 2 **3** **4** **5** **6**	SL . 1 2 3 4 5 6
22	RI RH . 1 2 **3** 4 **5** **6** **7** 8 9 10	W WHST . 1 **2** 3 **4** **5** **6** **7** **8** **9** **10**	L LF . 1 2 3 **4** 5 6	SL . **1** **2** 3 **4** **5** **6**
23	RI RH . 1 2 **3** **4** **5** 6 **7** 8 9 10	W WHST . 1 **2** 3 **4** 5 6 7 8 9 10	L LF . 1 2 3 **4** **5** **6**	SL . 1 2 3 4 5 6
COMPLETE BOOK	RI RH . **1** **2** **3** **4** **5** **6** **7** **8** **9** **10**	W WHST . **1** **2** **3** **4** **5** **6** **7** **8** **9** **10**	L LF . 1 **2** **3** **4** **5** **6**	SL . **1** **2** 3 **4** **5** **6**

For the complete Common Core standard identifier, combine your grade + "." + letter code above + "." + number code above.

In addition to the correlations indicated here, the activities may be adapted or expanded to align to additional standards and to meet the diverse needs of your unique students!